An Order for
and Dedicati
after a Civil

Church House Publishing

Published by   Church House Publishing
                  Church House
                  Great Smith Street
                  London SW1P 3NZ

Copyright ©   *The Archbishops' Council 2000*

                  First published in this format 2001

                  0 7151 2062 X

Printed and bound by ArklePrint Ltd, Northampton
on 80 gsm Dutchman Ivory

Typeset by John Morgan and Shirley Thompson/Omnific
Designed by Derek Birdsall RDI

The material in this booklet is extracted from *Common Worship:
Pastoral Services*. It comprises:

¶   an Order for Prayer and Dedication after a Civil Marriage;
¶   extracts from Supplementary Texts to Marriage;
¶   Notes to an Order for Prayer and Dedication after a Civil Marriage.

Pagination   This booklet has two sets of page numbers. The outer numbers are
                  the booklet's own page numbers, while the inner numbers near the
                  centre of most pages refer to the equivalent pages in *Common
                  Worship: Pastoral Services*.

Contents

Notes

1 **The Nature of the Service**
The service is one in which the couple – already married –
wish to dedicate to God their life together. Because it is not a
marriage service, banns may not be called nor any entry made
in the Register of Marriages.

2 **Entrance of the Couple**
Husband and wife should enter the church together without
ceremony and sit together at the front of the church.

3 **The Prayers**
Other prayers may be used, especially when they form part of
the particular Christian tradition of the husband or wife.

4 **The Rings**
Because the marriage has already taken place, no ring is to be
given or received in the course of the service. If a ring is worn and
the prayer of blessing is to be used, the hand should be extended
towards the minister.

5 **The Minister**
When the service is not led by a priest, the Grace is used
in place of the Blessing.

6 **Holy Communion**
The structure of the Marriage Service within the Order for
the Celebration of Holy Communion should be followed. The
Introduction in this service replaces the Introduction; Prayers of
Penitence must be used; also, in the Liturgy of the Word, there
must be a Gospel reading, preceded by either one or two other
readings from Scripture and followed by a sermon. This is followed
by the Dedication and the Prayers, and the Liturgy of the Sacrament
follows. Any of the proper material in the Marriage Service within
the Order for the Celebration of Holy Communion may be used.

For General Rules for Regulating Authorized Forms of Service, see
Common Worship: Pastoral Services, *page 402.*

An Order for Prayer and Dedication after a Civil Marriage

For Notes, see page iv.

Introduction

A hymn may be sung.

The minister may welcome the people and then says

The Lord be with you

All **and also with you.**

Preface

N and N, you stand in the presence of God as man and wife to dedicate to him your life together, that he may consecrate your marriage and empower you to keep the covenant and promise you have solemnly declared.

[The Bible teaches us that marriage is a gift of God in creation and a means of his grace, a holy mystery in which man and woman become one flesh. It is God's purpose that, as husband and wife give themselves to each other in love throughout their lives, they shall be united in that love as Christ is united with his Church.

Marriage is given, that husband and wife may comfort and help each other, living faithfully together in need and in plenty, in sorrow and in joy. It is given, that with delight and tenderness they may know each other in love, and, through the joy of their bodily union, may strengthen the union of their hearts and lives. It is given as the foundation of family life in which children may be [born and] nurtured in accordance with God's will, to his praise and glory. This is the meaning of the marriage you have made.]

You now wish to affirm your desire to live as followers of Christ, and you have come to him, the fountain of grace, that, strengthened by the prayers of the Church, you may be enabled to fulfil your marriage vows in love and faithfulness.

Let us keep silence and remember God's presence with us now.

God is love, and those who live in love live in God
and God lives in them.   *1 John 4.16*

All   **Almighty God,**
to whom all hearts are open,
all desires known,
and from whom no secrets are hidden:
cleanse the thoughts of our hearts
by the inspiration of your Holy Spirit,
that we may perfectly love you,
and worthily magnify your holy name;
through Christ our Lord.
Amen.

Prayers of Penitence

The following Summary of the Law may be said

Our Lord Jesus Christ said:
The first commandment is this:
'Hear, O Israel, the Lord our God is the only Lord.
You shall love the Lord your God with all your heart,
with all your soul, with all your mind,
and with all your strength.'

The second is this: 'Love your neighbour as yourself.'
There is no other commandment greater than these.
On these two commandments hang all the law and the prophets.

All   **Amen. Lord, have mercy.**

A minister may use these or other suitable words

God so loved the world
that he gave his only Son Jesus Christ
to save us from our sins,
to be our advocate in heaven,
and to bring us to eternal life.

Let us confess our sins in penitence and faith,
firmly resolved to keep God's commandments
and to live in love and peace with all.

(or)

We come to God as one from whom no secrets are hidden,
to ask for his forgiveness and peace.

Either

All **Lord our God,**
in our sin we have avoided your call.
Our love for you is like a morning cloud,
like the dew that goes away early.
Have mercy on us;
deliver us from judgement;
bind up our wounds and revive us;
in Jesus Christ our Lord.
Amen.

The minister says

The Lord forgive *you your* sin,
unite *you* in the love which took Christ to the cross,
and bring *you* in the Spirit to his wedding feast in heaven.

All **Amen.**

(or)

Lord, in our weakness you are our strength.
Lord, have mercy.

All **Lord, have mercy.**

Lord, when we stumble, you raise us up.
Christ, have mercy.

All **Christ, have mercy.**

Lord, when we fail, you give us new life.
Lord, have mercy.

All **Lord, have mercy.**

The minister says

May God in his goodness forgive *us our* sins,
grant *us* strength in *our* weakness,
and bring *us* to eternal life,
through Jesus Christ our Lord.

All **Amen.**

The Collect

The minister invites the people to pray, silence is kept and the minister says the Collect

God our Father,
you have taught us through your Son
that love is the fulfilling of the law.
Grant to your servants
that, loving one another,
they may continue in your love until their lives' end:
through Jesus Christ your Son our Lord,
who is alive and reigns with you,
in the unity of the Holy Spirit,
one God, now and for ever.

All   **Amen.**

Readings

At least one reading from the Bible is used. A selection of readings is found on pages 11–23.

If there are two readings, a psalm or a hymn may be sung between them.

A sermon may be preached here or after the Dedication.

The Dedication

The husband and wife face the minister, who says

N and N, you have committed yourselves to each other in marriage,
and your marriage is recognized by law.
The Church of Christ understands marriage to be,
in the will of God,
the union of a man and a woman,
for better, for worse,
for richer, for poorer,
in sickness and in health,
to love and to cherish,
till parted by death.
Is this your understanding of the covenant and promise
    that you have made?

*Husband
and wife*   It is.

The minister says to the husband

N, have you resolved to be faithful to your wife,
forsaking all others,
so long as you both shall live?

Husband   That is my resolve, with the help of God.

The minister says to the wife

N, have you resolved to be faithful to your husband,
forsaking all others,
so long as you both shall live?

Wife   That is my resolve, with the help of God.

The minister may say

Heavenly Father, by your blessing
let *these rings* be to N and N
a symbol of unending love and faithfulness
and of the promises they have made to each other;
through Jesus Christ our Lord.

All   **Amen.**

N and N have here affirmed
their Christian understanding and resolve
in the marriage which they have begun.
Will you, their families and friends,
support and uphold them in their marriage,
now and in the years to come?

All   **We will.**

The congregation remains standing.

The husband and wife kneel and say together

Heavenly Father,
we offer you our souls and bodies,
our thoughts and words and deeds,
our love for one another.
Unite our wills in your will,
that we may grow together
in love and peace
all the days of our life;
through Jesus Christ our Lord. Amen.

The minister says

Almighty God give you grace to persevere,
that he may complete in you
the work he has already begun,
through Jesus Christ our Lord.

All   **Amen.**

The Lord bless and watch over you,
the Lord make his face shine upon you
and be gracious to you,
the Lord look kindly on you and give you peace
all the days of your life.

All   **Amen.**

A sermon may be preached.

A hymn may be sung.

Prayers

One or more of the following prayers may be used

Almighty God,
you send your Holy Spirit
to be the life and light of all your people.
Open the hearts of these your servants to the riches of his grace,
that they may bring forth the fruit of the Spirit
in love and joy and peace;
through Jesus Christ our Lord.

All **Amen.**

For the gift of children

Heavenly Father,
maker of all things,
you enable us to share in your work of creation.
Bless this couple in the gift and care of children,
that their home may be a place of love, security and truth
and their children grow up to know and love you in your Son
Jesus Christ our Lord.

All **Amen.**

For families

Father of all life,
whose promise is to be the God of all the families of your people,
give your grace to *N* and *N* in their new life together
and bless those for whom they care.
Enfold them in your love
as they share in their new family,
that they may grow up in all things into Christ,
who gave himself that all humanity might be made one in him.

All **Amen.**

Heavenly Father,
we are your children, made in your image.
Hear our prayer
that fathers and mothers, sons and daughters,
may find together the perfect love that casts out fear,
walk together in the way that leads to eternal life
and grow up together into the full humanity
of your Son Jesus Christ our Lord.

All   **Amen.**

Concluding prayer
Eternal God, true and loving Father,
in holy marriage you make your servants one.
May their life together witness to your love in this troubled world;
may unity overcome division,
forgiveness heal injury
and joy triumph over sorrow,
through Jesus Christ our Lord.

All   **Amen.**

As our Saviour taught us, so we pray

All   **Our Father in heaven,**
hallowed be your name,
your kingdom come,
your will be done,
on earth as in heaven.
Give us today our daily bread.
Forgive us our sins
as we forgive those who sin against us.
Lead us not into temptation
but deliver us from evil.
For the kingdom, the power,
and the glory are yours
now and for ever.
Amen.

(or)

Let us pray with confidence as our Saviour has taught us

All   **Our Father, who art in heaven,**
hallowed be thy name;
thy kingdom come;
thy will be done;
on earth as it is in heaven.
Give us this day our daily bread.
And forgive us our trespasses,
as we forgive those who trespass against us.
And lead us not into temptation;
but deliver us from evil.
For thine is the kingdom,
the power and the glory,
for ever and ever.
Amen.

A hymn may be sung.

God the Holy Trinity make *you* strong in faith and love,
defend *you* on every side, and guide *you* in truth and peace;
and the blessing of God almighty,
the Father, the Son, and the Holy Spirit,
be among *you* and remain with *you* always.

All **Amen.**

Any suitable translation may be used.

Old Testament and Apocrypha

Genesis 1.26-28

Then God said, 'Let us make humankind in our image, according to our likeness; and let them have dominion over the fish of the sea, and over the birds of the air, and over the cattle, and over all the wild animals of the earth, and over every creeping thing that creeps upon the earth.'

So God created humankind in his image,
in the image of God he created them;
male and female he created them.

God blessed them, and God said to them, 'Be fruitful and multiply, and fill the earth and subdue it; and have dominion over the fish of the sea and over the birds of the air and over every living thing that moves upon the earth.'

Song of Solomon 2.10-13; 8.6,7

My beloved speaks and says to me:
'Arise, my love, my fair one,
and come away;
for now the winter is past,
the rain is over and gone.
The flowers appear on the earth;
the time of singing has come,
and the voice of the turtle dove
is heard in our land.
The fig tree puts forth its figs,
and the vines are in blossom;
they give forth fragrance.
Arise, my love, my fair one,
and come away.'

Set me as a seal upon your heart,
as a seal upon your arm;
for love is strong as death,
passion fierce as the grave.
Its flashes are flashes of fire,
a raging flame.
Many waters cannot quench love,
neither can floods drown it.
If one offered for love
all the wealth of one's house,
it would be utterly scorned.

Jeremiah 31.31-34

The days are surely coming, says the Lord, when I will make a
new covenant with the house of Israel and the house of Judah.
It will not be like the covenant that I made with their ancestors
when I took them by the hand to bring them out of the land of
Egypt – a covenant that they broke, though I was their husband,
says the Lord. But this is the covenant that I will make with the
house of Israel after those days, says the Lord: I will put my law
within them, and I will write it on their hearts; and I will be their
God, and they shall be my people. No longer shall they teach one
another, or say to each other, 'Know the Lord', for they shall all
know me, from the least of them to the greatest, says the Lord;
for I will forgive their iniquity, and remember their sin no more.

Tobit 8.4-8

When the parents had gone out and shut the door of the room,
Tobias got out of bed and said to Sarah, 'Sister, get up, and let us
pray and implore our Lord that he grant us mercy and safety.'
So she got up, and they began to pray and implore that they might
be kept safe. Tobias began by saying,
'Blessed are you, O God of our ancestors,
and blessed is your name in all generations for ever.
Let the heavens and the whole creation bless you for ever.
You made Adam, and for him you made his wife Eve
as a helper and support.
From the two of them the human race has sprung.
You said, "It is not good that the man should be alone;
let us make a helper for him like himself."

I now am taking this kinswoman of mine,
not because of lust,
but with sincerity.
Grant that she and I may find mercy
and that we may grow old together.'

And they both said, 'Amen, amen.'

Epistle

Romans 7.1,2,9-18

Do you not know, brothers and sisters — for I am speaking to those who know the law — that the law is binding on a person only during that person's lifetime? Thus a married woman is bound by the law to her husband as long as he lives; but if her husband dies, she is discharged from the law concerning the husband.

I was once alive apart from the law, but when the commandment came, sin revived and I died, and the very commandment that promised life proved to be death to me. For sin, seizing an opportunity in the commandment, deceived me and through it killed me. So the law is holy, and the commandment is holy and just and good.

Did what is good, then, bring death to me? By no means! It was sin, working death in me through what is good, in order that sin might be shown to be sin, and through the commandment might become sinful beyond measure.

For we know that the law is spiritual; but I am of the flesh, sold into slavery under sin. I do not understand my own actions. For I do not do what I want, but I do the very thing I hate. Now if I do what I do not want, I agree that the law is good. But in fact it is no longer I that do it, but sin that dwells within me. For I know that nothing good dwells within me, that is, in my flesh. I can will what is right, but I cannot do it.

Romans 8.31-35,37-39

What then are we to say about these things? If God is for us, who is against us? He who did not withhold his own Son, but gave him up for all of us, will he not with him also give us everything else? Who will bring any charge against God's elect? It is God who justifies. Who is to condemn? It is Christ Jesus, who died, yes, who was raised, who is at the right hand of God, who indeed intercedes for us. Who will separate us from the love of Christ? Will hardship, or distress, or persecution, or famine, or nakedness, or peril, or sword?

No, in all these things we are more than conquerors through him who loved us. For I am convinced that neither death, nor life, nor angels, nor rulers, nor things present, nor things to come, nor powers, nor height, nor depth, nor anything else in all creation, will be able to separate us from the love of God in Christ Jesus our Lord.

Romans 12.1,2,9-13

I appeal to you therefore, brothers and sisters, by the mercies of God, to present your bodies as a living sacrifice, holy and acceptable to God, which is your spiritual worship. Do not be conformed to this world, but be transformed by the renewing of your minds, so that you may discern what is the will of God – what is good and acceptable and perfect.

Let love be genuine; hate what is evil, hold fast to what is good; love one another with mutual affection; outdo one another in showing honour. Do not lag in zeal, be ardent in spirit, serve the Lord. Rejoice in hope, be patient in suffering, persevere in prayer. Contribute to the needs of the saints; extend hospitality to strangers.

Romans 15.1-3,5-7,13

We who are strong ought to put up with the failings of the weak, and not to please ourselves. Each of us must please our neighbour for the good purpose of building up the neighbour. For Christ did not please himself; but, as it is written, 'The insults of those who insult you have fallen on me.'

May the God of steadfastness and encouragement grant you to live in harmony with one another, in accordance with Christ Jesus, so that together you may with one voice glorify the God and Father of our Lord Jesus Christ. Welcome one another, therefore, just as Christ has welcomed you, for the glory of God.

May the God of hope fill you with all joy and peace in believing, so that you may abound in hope by the power of the Holy Spirit.

1 Corinthians 13

If I speak in the tongues of mortals and of angels, but do not have love, I am a noisy gong or a clanging cymbal. And if I have prophetic powers, and understand all mysteries and all knowledge, and if I have all faith, so as to remove mountains, but do not have love, I am nothing. If I give away all my possessions, and if I hand over my body so that I may boast, but do not have love, I gain nothing.

Love is patient; love is kind; love is not envious or boastful or arrogant or rude. It does not insist on its own way; it is not irritable or resentful; it does not rejoice in wrongdoing, but rejoices in the truth. It bears all things, believes all things, hopes all things, endures all things.

Love never ends. But as for prophecies, they will come to an end; as for tongues, they will cease; as for knowledge, it will come to an end. For we know only in part, and we prophesy only in part; but when the complete comes, the partial will come to an end. When I was a child, I spoke like a child, I thought like a child, I reasoned like a child; when I became an adult, I put an end to childish ways. For now we see in a mirror, dimly, but then we will see face to face. Now I know only in part; then I will know fully, even as I have been fully known. And now faith, hope, and love abide, these three; and the greatest of these is love.

Ephesians 3.14-end

I bow my knees before the Father, from whom every family in heaven and on earth takes its name. I pray that, according to the riches of his glory, he may grant that you may be strengthened in your inner being with power through his Spirit, and that Christ may dwell in your hearts through faith, as you are being rooted and grounded in love. I pray that you may have the power to comprehend, with all the saints, what is the breadth and length and height and depth, and to know the love of Christ that surpasses knowledge, so that you may be filled with all the fullness of God.

Now to him who by the power at work within us is able to accomplish abundantly far more than all we can ask or imagine, to him be glory in the church and in Christ Jesus to all generations, for ever and ever. Amen.

Ephesians 4.1-6

I, the prisoner in the Lord, beg you to lead a life worthy of the calling to which you have been called, with all humility and gentleness, with patience, bearing with one another in love, making every effort to maintain the unity of the Spirit in the bond of peace. There is one body and one Spirit, just as you were called to the one hope of your calling, one Lord, one faith, one baptism, one God and Father of all, who is above all and through all and in all.

Ephesians 5.21-end

Be subject to one another out of reverence for Christ.

Wives, be subject to your husbands as you are to the Lord. For the husband is the head of the wife just as Christ is the head of the church, the body of which he is the Saviour. Just as the church is subject to Christ, so also wives ought to be, in everything, to their husbands.

Husbands, love your wives, just as Christ loved the church and gave himself up for her, in order to make her holy by cleansing her with the washing of water by the word, so as to present the church to himself in splendour, without a spot or wrinkle or anything of the kind – yes, so that she may be holy and without blemish. In the same way, husbands should love their wives as they do their own bodies. He who loves his wife loves himself. For no one ever hates his own body, but he nourishes and tenderly cares for it, just as Christ does for the church, because we are members of his body. 'For this reason a man will leave his father and mother and be joined to his wife, and the two will become one flesh.' This is a great mystery, and I am applying it to Christ and the church. Each of you, however, should love his wife as himself, and a wife should respect her husband.

Philippians 4.4-9

Rejoice in the Lord always; again I will say, Rejoice. Let your gentleness be known to everyone. The Lord is near. Do not worry about anything, but in everything by prayer and supplication with thanksgiving let your requests be made known to God. And the peace of God, which surpasses all understanding, will guard your hearts and your minds in Christ Jesus.

Finally, beloved, whatever is true, whatever is honourable, whatever is just, whatever is pure, whatever is pleasing, whatever is commendable, if there is any excellence and if there is anything worthy of praise, think about these things. Keep on doing the things that you have learned and received and heard and seen in me, and the God of peace will be with you.

Colossians 3.12-17

As God's chosen ones, holy and beloved, clothe yourselves with compassion, kindness, humility, meekness, and patience. Bear with one another and, if anyone has a complaint against another, forgive each other; just as the Lord has forgiven you, so you also must forgive. Above all, clothe yourselves with love, which binds everything together in perfect harmony. And let the peace of Christ rule in your hearts, to which indeed you were called in the one body. And be thankful. Let the word of Christ dwell in you richly; teach and admonish one another in all wisdom; and with gratitude in your hearts sing psalms, hymns, and spiritual songs to God. And whatever you do, in word or deed, do everything in the name of the Lord Jesus, giving thanks to God the Father through him.

Little children, let us love, not in word or speech, but in truth and action. And by this we will know that we are from the truth and will reassure our hearts before him whenever our hearts condemn us; for God is greater than our hearts, and he knows everything. Beloved, if our hearts do not condemn us, we have boldness before God; and we receive from him whatever we ask, because we obey his commandments and do what pleases him.

And this is his commandment, that we should believe in the name of his Son Jesus Christ and love one another, just as he has commanded us. All who obey his commandments abide in him, and he abides in them. And by this we know that he abides in us, by the Spirit that he has given us.

1 John 4.7-12

Beloved, let us love one another, because love is from God; everyone who loves is born of God and knows God. Whoever does not love does not know God, for God is love. God's love was revealed among us in this way: God sent his only Son into the world so that we might live through him. In this is love, not that we loved God but that he loved us and sent his Son to be the atoning sacrifice for our sins. Beloved, since God loved us so much, we also ought to love one another. No one has ever seen God; if we love one another, God lives in us, and his love is perfected in us.

Gospel

Matthew 5.1-10

When Jesus saw the crowds, he went up the mountain; and after
he sat down, his disciples came to him. Then he began to speak,
and taught them, saying:

'Blessed are the poor in spirit, for theirs is the kingdom of heaven.
Blessed are those who mourn, for they will be comforted.
Blessed are the meek, for they will inherit the earth.
Blessed are those who hunger and thirst for righteousness,
     for they will be filled.
Blessed are the merciful, for they will receive mercy.
Blessed are the pure in heart, for they will see God.
Blessed are the peacemakers, for they will be called children of God.
Blessed are those who are persecuted for righteousness' sake,
     for theirs is the kingdom of heaven.'

Matthew 7.21,24-end

Jesus said, 'Not everyone who says to me, "Lord, Lord", will enter
the kingdom of heaven, but only one who does the will of my
Father in heaven.

'Everyone then who hears these words of mine and acts on them
will be like a wise man who built his house on rock. The rain fell,
the floods came, and the winds blew and beat on that house, but it
did not fall, because it had been founded on rock. And everyone who
hears these words of mine and does not act on them will be like a
foolish man who built his house on sand. The rain fell, and the floods
came, and the winds blew and beat against that house, and it fell –
and great was its fall!'

Now when Jesus had finished saying these things, the crowds
were astounded at his teaching, for he taught them as one having
authority, and not as their scribes.

Jesus said, 'From the beginning of creation, "God made them male
and female." "For this reason a man shall leave his father and mother
and be joined to his wife, and the two shall become one flesh."
So they are no longer two, but one flesh. Therefore what God has
joined together, let no one separate.'

People were bringing little children to him in order that he might
touch them; and the disciples spoke sternly to them. But when Jesus
saw this, he was indignant and said to them, 'Let the little children
come to me; do not stop them; for it is to such as these that the
kingdom of God belongs. Truly I tell you, whoever does not receive
the kingdom of God as a little child will never enter it.' And he took
them up in his arms, laid his hands on them, and blessed them.

On the third day there was a wedding in Cana of Galilee, and the
mother of Jesus was there. Jesus and his disciples had also been
invited to the wedding. When the wine gave out, the mother of
Jesus said to him, 'They have no wine.' And Jesus said to her,
'Woman, what concern is that to you and to me? My hour has not
yet come.' His mother said to the servants, 'Do whatever he tells
you.' Now standing there were six stone water-jars for the Jewish
rites of purification, each holding twenty or thirty gallons. Jesus
said to them, 'Fill the jars with water.' And they filled them up to
the brim. He said to them, 'Now draw some out, and take it to the
chief steward.' So they took it. When the steward tasted the water
that had become wine, and did not know where it came from
(though the servants who had drawn the water knew), the steward
called the bridegroom and said to him, 'Everyone serves the good
wine first, and then the inferior wine after the guests have become
drunk. But you have kept the good wine until now.' Jesus did this,
the first of his signs, in Cana of Galilee, and revealed his glory; and
his disciples believed in him.

John 15.1-8

Jesus said to his disciples: 'I am the true vine, and my Father is the vinegrower. He removes every branch in me that bears no fruit. Every branch that bears fruit he prunes to make it bear more fruit. You have already been cleansed by the word that I have spoken to you. Abide in me as I abide in you. Just as the branch cannot bear fruit by itself unless it abides in the vine, neither can you unless you abide in me. I am the vine, you are the branches. Those who abide in me and I in them bear much fruit, because apart from me you can do nothing. Whoever does not abide in me is thrown away like a branch and withers; such branches are gathered, thrown into the fire, and burned. If you abide in me, and my words abide in you, ask for whatever you wish, and it will be done for you. My Father is glorified by this, that you bear much fruit and become my disciples.'

John 15.9-17

Jesus said to his disciples: 'As the Father has loved me, so I have loved you; abide in my love. If you keep my commandments, you will abide in my love, just as I have kept my Father's commandments and abide in his love. I have said these things to you so that my joy may be in you, and that your joy may be complete.

This is my commandment, that you love one another as I have loved you. No one has greater love than this, to lay down one's life for one's friends. You are my friends if you do what I command you. I do not call you servants any longer, because the servant does not know what the master is doing; but I have called you friends, because I have made known to you everything that I have heard from my Father. You did not choose me but I chose you. And I appointed you to go and bear fruit, fruit that will last, so that the Father will give you whatever you ask him in my name. I am giving you these commands so that you may love one another.'

Psalms

1   God be gracious to us and bless us ✦
     and make his face to shine upon us,

2   That your way may be known upon earth, ✦
     your saving power among all nations.

3   *Let the peoples praise you, O God;* ✦
     let all the peoples praise you.

4   O let the nations rejoice and be glad, ✦
     for you will judge the peoples righteously
          and govern the nations upon earth.

5   *Let the peoples praise you, O God;* ✦
     let all the peoples praise you.

6   Then shall the earth bring forth her increase, ✦
     and God, our own God, will bless us.

7   God will bless us, ✦
     and all the ends of the earth shall fear him.

Psalm 121

1   I lift up my eyes to the hills; ✦
     from where is my help to come?

2   My help comes from the Lord, ✦
     the maker of heaven and earth.

3   He will not suffer your foot to stumble; ✦
     he who watches over you will not sleep.

4   Behold, he who keeps watch over Israel ✦
     shall neither slumber nor sleep.

5   The Lord himself watches over you; ✦
     the Lord is your shade at your right hand,

6   So that the sun shall not strike you by day, ✦
     neither the moon by night.

7   The Lord shall keep you from all evil; ✦
     it is he who shall keep your soul.

8   The Lord shall keep watch over your going out
          and your coming in, ✦
     from this time forth for evermore.

1   Unless the Lord builds the house, ♦
     those who build it labour in vain.

2   Unless the Lord keeps the city, ♦
     the guard keeps watch in vain.

3   It is in vain that you hasten to rise up early
       and go so late to rest, eating the bread of toil, ♦
     for he gives his beloved sleep.

4   Children are a heritage from the Lord ♦
     and the fruit of the womb is his gift.

5   Like arrows in the hand of a warrior, ♦
     so are the children of one's youth.

6   Happy are those who have their quiver full of them: ♦
     they shall not be put to shame
       when they dispute with their enemies in the gate.

1   Blessed are all those who fear the Lord, ♦
     and walk in his ways.

2   You shall eat the fruit of the toil of your hands; ♦
     it shall go well with you, and happy shall you be.

3   Your wife within your house
       shall be like a fruitful vine; ♦
     your children round your table,
       like fresh olive branches.

4   Thus shall the one be blest ♦
     who fears the Lord.

5   The Lord from out of Zion bless you, ♦
     that you may see Jerusalem in prosperity
       all the days of your life.

6   May you see your children's children, ♦
     and may there be peace upon Israel.

A Song of Solomon

Refrain:

All **Many waters cannot quench love;**
neither can the floods drown it.

1   Set me as a seal upon your heart, ♦
    as a seal upon your arm;

2   For love is strong as death, passion fierce as the grave; ♦
    its flashes are flashes of fire, a raging flame.

3   Many waters cannot quench love, ♦
    neither can the floods drown it.

4   If all the wealth of our house were offered for love, ♦
    it would be utterly scorned.   *cf Song of Solomon 8.6-7*

    Glory to the Father and to the Son
    and to the Holy Spirit;
    as it was in the beginning is now
    and shall be for ever. Amen.

A Song of the Bride

Refrain:

All   **God makes righteousness and praise
blossom before all the nations.**

1   I will greatly rejoice in the Lord, ♦
my soul shall exult in my God;

2   Who has clothed me with the garments of salvation, ♦
and has covered me with the cloak of integrity,

3   As a bridegroom decks himself with a garland, ♦
and as a bride adorns herself with her jewels.

4   For as the earth puts forth her blossom, ♦
and as seeds in the garden spring up,

5   So shall God make righteousness and praise ♦
blossom before all the nations.

6   For Zion's sake I will not keep silent, ♦
and for Jerusalem's sake I will not rest,

7   Until her deliverance shines out like the dawn, ♦
and her salvation as a burning torch.

8   The nations shall see your deliverance, ♦
and all rulers shall see your glory;

9   Then you shall be called by a new name ♦
which the mouth of God will give.

10   You shall be a crown of glory in the hand of the Lord, ♦
a royal diadem in the hand of your God.   *Isaiah 61.10,11; 62.1-3*

Glory to the Father and to the Son
and to the Holy Spirit;
as it was in the beginning is now
and shall be for ever. Amen.

Magnificat (The Song of Mary)

1   My soul proclaims the greatness of the Lord,
           my spirit rejoices in God my Saviour; ♦
    he has looked with favour on his lowly servant.

2   From this day all generations will call me blessed; ♦
    the Almighty has done great things for me
           and holy is his name.

3   He has mercy on those who fear him, ♦
    from generation to generation.

4   He has shown strength with his arm ♦
    and has scattered the proud in their conceit,

5   Casting down the mighty from their thrones ♦
    and lifting up the lowly.

6   He has filled the hungry with good things ♦
    and sent the rich away empty.

7   He has come to the aid of his servant Israel, ♦
    to remember his promise of mercy,

8   The promise made to our ancestors, ♦
    to Abraham and his children for ever.   *Luke 1.46-55*

    Glory to the Father and to the Son
    and to the Holy Spirit;
    as it was in the beginning is now
    and shall be for ever. Amen.

A Song of the Lamb

Refrain:

All **Let us rejoice and exult
and give glory and homage to our God.**

1   Salvation and glory and power belong to our God, ♦
    whose judgements are true and just.

2   Praise our God, all you his servants, ♦
    all who fear him, both small and great.

3   The Lord our God, the Almighty, reigns: ♦
    let us rejoice and exult and give him the glory.

4   For the marriage of the Lamb has come ♦
    and his bride has made herself ready.

5   Blessed are those who are invited ♦
    to the wedding banquet of the Lamb.   *Revelation 19.1b,2b,5b,6b,7,9b*

To the One who sits on the throne and to the Lamb ♦
be blessing and honour and glory and might,
    for ever and ever. Amen.

Authorization

¶ An Order for Prayer and Dedication after a Civil Marriage and the
   Canticles have been commended by the House of Bishops of the
   General Synod pursuant to Canon B 2 of the Canons of the Church
   of England and are published with the agreement of the House.

   Under Canon B 4 it is open to each bishop to authorize, if he sees
   fit, the form of service to be used within his diocese. He may specify
   that the services shall be those commended by the House, or that a
   diocesan form of them shall be used. If the bishop gives no
   directions in this matter the priest remains free, subject to the
   terms of Canon B 5, to make use of the services as commended by
   the House.

¶ The Readings and Psalms are authorized pursuant to Canon B 2 of
   the Canons of the Church of England for use until further resolution
   of the General Synod.

Acknowledgements

*The publisher gratefully acknowledges permission to reproduce copyright
material in this book. Every effort has been made to trace and contact
copyright holders. If there are any inadvertent omissions we apologize to
those concerned and undertake to include suitable acknowledgements in
all future editions.*

Published sources include the following:

Cambridge University Press: Extracts (and adapted extracts) from
The Book of Common Prayer, the rights in which are vested in the
Crown, are reproduced by permission of the Crown's Patentee,
Cambridge University Press.

The Division of Christian Education of the National Council of
Churches in the USA: Unless otherwise stated, Scripture quotations
are from *The New Revised Standard Version of the Bible*, copyright ©
1989 by the Division of Christian Education of the National Council
of Churches in the USA. Used by permission. All rights reserved.

The English Language Liturgical Consultation: English translation of
Gloria in excelsis, the Lord's Prayer and Magnificat prepared by the
English Language Liturgical Consultation, based on (or excerpted
from) *Praying Together*, copyright © ELLC 1988.